D1109566

GREEK BEASTS AND HEROES

The Flying Horse

You can read the stories in the
Greek Beasts and Heroes series in any order.

If you'd like to read more about some of the
characters in this book, turn to pages 76-78
to find out which other books to try.

Atticus's journey continues on
from *The Fire Breather*.

To find out where he goes next,
read *The Harp of Death*.

Turn to page 79 for a complete
list of titles in the series.

GREEK BEASTS AND HEROES

The Flying Horse

LUCY COATS
Illustrated by Anthony Lewis

Orion
Children's Books

Text and illustrations first appeared in
Atticus the Storyteller's 100 Greek Myths
First published in Great Britain in 2002
by Orion Children's Books
This edition published in Great Britain in 2010
by Orion Children's Books
a division of the Orion Publishing Group Ltd
Orion House
5 Upper St Martin's Lane
London WC2H 9EA
An Hachette UK company

1 3 5 7 9 8 6 4 2

The Orion Publishing Group's policy is to use papers that are natural,
renewable and recyclable products and made from wood grown in sustainable
forests. The logging and manufacturing processes are expected to conform
to the environmental regulations of the country of origin.

A catalogue record for this book is available from the British Library

ISBN 978 1 4440 0071 9

Printed in China

www.orionbooks.co.uk
www.lucycoats.com

For my darling Tabbi,
because she wanted one all to herself,
with love.

L. C.

For Vicky and Adie

A. L.

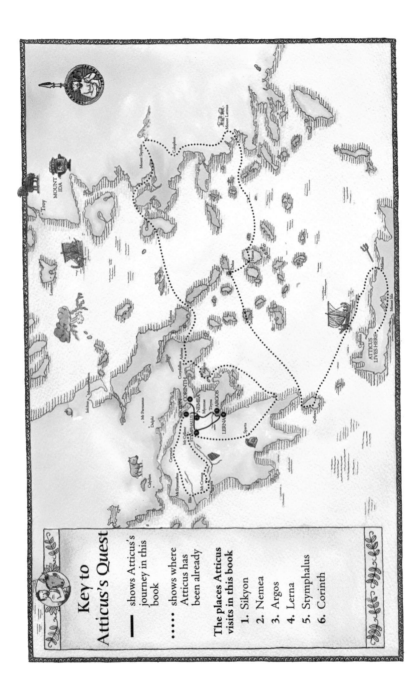

Key to Atticus's Quest

— shows Atticus's journey in this book

····· shows where Atticus has been already

The places Atticus visits in this book

1. Sikyon
2. Nemea
3. Argos
4. Lerna
5. Stymphalus
6. Corinth

Contents

Stories from the Heavens

Long ago, in ancient Greece, gods and goddesses, heroes and heroines lived together with fearful monsters and every kind of fabulous beast that ever flew, or walked or swam. But little by little, as people began to build more villages and towns and cities, the gods and monsters disappeared into the secret places of the world and the heavens, so that they could have some peace.

Before they
disappeared,
the gods and
goddesses gave
the gift of storytelling to men and women,
so that nobody would ever forget them.
They ordered that there should be a great
storytelling festival once every seven
years on the slopes of Mount Ida, near
Troy, and that tellers of tales should
come from all over Greece and from

 lands near and far to take
part. Every seven years a
beautiful painted vase,
filled to the brim with
gold, magically appeared as a first prize,
and the winner was honoured for the rest
of his life by all the people of Greece.

Loud roaring noises were coming from the rocks above Nemea as they made camp.

"What's that?" asked Agathon, the youngest member of the players.

"It's a mountain lion," said Atticus. "Don't worry, he won't come near our fire."

"Tell us the story of Heracles and the lion, Atticus," called Glaucus. "It'll take young Agathon's mind off tomorrow's performance. He's got to sing a solo!"

The Magic Skin

The very first task that Heracles ever had to perform for King Eurystheus was to kill the Nemean lion. This lion was one of the children of the terrible monsters Echidna and Typhon, and it was a most dreadful beast.

Heracles met no one on his way to Nemea – the lion had devoured them all – so he had to search for a long time before he found the lion's cave.

When he did find it, the lion was just returning after a day's hunting.

He was covered in blood, and flies were buzzing after him as he padded along on his huge paws, swishing his tail like a cat. Heracles hid in a bush and shot several sharp arrows at him. But to his surprise the arrows bounced off, and the lion just yawned and lay down to sleep off his meal.

Heracles yelled and charged at him with his sword. It was the strongest sword ever made, but the lion's hide was so tough that it just bent and broke as if it was made of wax.

The lion didn't even wake up.

Heracles had only one weapon left – the twisted, knotted club he had had as a boy for protecting his sheep. It was covered in sharp metal spikes, and Heracles lifted

 13

it over his shoulders and brought it smashing down on the lion's head.

The lion growled and shook his head a little because his ears were ringing, and then he retired into the cave to finish his interrupted sleep.

Heracles looked at the splintered piece of wood in his hands. Whatever could he do? The lion couldn't be killed with any weapon, that was obvious. Heracles would just have to rely on his own strength.

He ran into the cave and jumped onto the sleeping lion's back.

He put his huge hands round the lion's neck and began to squeeze.

At this, the lion woke up, and began to thrash and roar and roll around the cave floor. But Heracles didn't let go until he was dead.

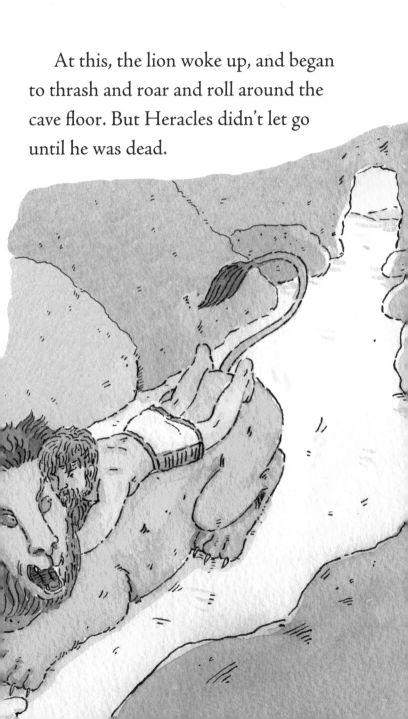

The people of Tiryns gasped as they saw the lion draped round Heracles' neck. He walked straight into the throne room, and dumped the dead animal at Eurystheus's feet.

"Ugh!" shrieked Eurystheus, running behind a curtain. "Take it away."

So Heracles took it away and skinned it with its own sharp claws, and made the skin into armour, which nothing could penetrate. He made the head into a helmet, which he wore whenever he went into battle.

It was after this that the cowardly Eurystheus ordered a great bronze jar to be made, and he decided to hide in it if ever Heracles should bring such a fearsome beast near him again.

Atticus and the others had stopped in
Mycenae to watch a juggler while Glaucus
found a place to stay. They had been walking
for days, and they were all tired of camping
on the hard ground. The journey to Corinth
was taking a long time in the summer heat.

The juggler threw three brass balls
high in the air. One fell, and rolled to a
stop at Atticus's feet.

"That's me done for the day," said
the juggler as Atticus handed it to him.
"It's thirsty work."

"Come and have a drink with us," said
Atticus. "Your juggling reminded me of
Hera's golden apples. You can listen to
the story with my friends."

The Golden Apples

Heracles had finished his tasks in exactly eight years and a month.

"Can I go now?" he asked. Eurystheus smiled nastily.

"Oh, I don't think so. Not just yet," he said. "Hera says you ought to do two more things for me, because Iolaus helped you with the Hydra, and you let the two rivers clean out Augeias' stables for you."

Heracles sighed.

Then Eurystheus ordered Heracles to pick him three golden apples from Hera's secret garden as his eleventh task.

"No one knows the way," he grinned,

 19

"except one person. And I'm not telling you who it is, so there."

Luckily, Heracles already knew that the only person who could tell him how to get to Hera's garden was Nereus, the Old Man of the Sea.

After a long journey, he tiptoed up to the mouth of the river Po, where Nereus was taking a nap among the seaweed.

"Got you!" he cried, seizing the god in his strong arms.

Nereus woke up with a jump and

turned into a hissing snake. Then he turned quickly into a lion, a tiny mouse, a worm, a speck of dust and a raging fire.

But Heracles held on, never letting go, and finally Nereus turned back into himself.

"What do you want?" he asked grumpily.

Heracles told him.

"Ho!" said Nereus. "You want to be careful picking those apples. Only gods can go into that garden. Atlas lives round there – why don't you ask him to help?"

Then he gave Heracles directions and went back to his seaweed bed.

"And don't come disturbing me again, or I'll turn you into something!" he snarled as he closed his eyes.

 21

Heracles took six months to reach Hera's garden, and he had many adventures getting there.

On the way, he passed Prometheus, still chained to his crag in the Caucasus, and still having his liver torn out by the giant eagle every morning.

When Heracles heard his groans, he went to visit him. "Poor old chap," he said sympathetically. "How long is it that you've been here?"

"Thirty thousand years," moaned Prometheus.

Heracles took aim at the eagle and shot it dead, then he took his knobbly club, and started to bash and bang at Prometheus's chains.

"It's far too long," said Heracles. "I'm sure Zeus has forgiven you by now."

And he was quite right, Zeus had, because Prometheus had given him some very good advice over the years. But he commanded that Prometheus should always wear a chain set with stones from his mountain, so that he would never forget his crime.

When Heracles reached Hera's garden in the farthest west, he found it was surrounded by a high wall.

He looked over the top, and there was a beautiful tree, with shining golden apples dangling from its branches in the light of the setting sun.

Three nymphs in gauzy dresses were dancing round the tree, watched by an enormous dragon with a hundred heads, which had been set to guard the tree by Hera when her other monster, Argos, had been killed by Hermes.

As Heracles turned to go and find Atlas to help him, he saw a giant hand propping up the sky, just where it curved away on the horizon.

When Heracles got nearer, he found

Atlas holding up the whole heavens on his shoulders.

"Looks heavy," he said.

Atlas nodded, and the sky spilled a few stars. "It is," he grunted. "Perhaps you'd like to have a go. You look a strong man, and I could do with a rest."

Heracles nodded. "I'll do it if you go and pick me three of those golden apples over there," he agreed.

But Atlas looked worried. "Is that dreadful dragon, Ladon, still there?" he asked.

Heracles nodded again. "Well, I won't do it unless you kill him for me. Those hundred heads give me the creeps."

 26

So Heracles crept back to the garden and shot Ladon in the heart with one of his deadly poisoned arrows.

The dragon died so quietly that the nymphs didn't even notice.

Heracles swapped places with Atlas, who soon returned with the golden apples.

 27

"You look very comfortable," said Atlas, who was enjoying his freedom. "Tell you what! I'll take the apples to King Eurystheus and you stay here for a bit." A crafty gleam came into his eye. "I promise to come back as soon as I've delivered them!"

Heracles could see that Atlas was lying, so he thought he would play a trick on him. The sky was getting very heavy, and he couldn't possibly hold it up for another minute.

"I'll need a pad for my shoulders, then," Heracles said quickly. "Just hold the sky up a second while I run and get one."

Atlas put the apples on the ground and shouldered his burden once more.

"Sorry, Atlas," said Heracles. "But I really have to go now!"

And picking up the apples, he ran off as fast as he could, with Atlas's roars ringing in his ears.

Eurystheus was amazed when he saw the golden apples.

"I can't keep them here," he blustered. "Take them away – they're terribly dangerous!"

So Heracles went to find Athene, who took the apples back to Hera's garden and hung them on the tree again.

 29

And there they hang to this day, sparkling in the sunset light as the three nymphs dance and play around them.

"Three jars of wine, six obols' worth of olives, ten loaves of bread, and a whole cheese, please," said Atticus, stopping at a stall in the market square in Tiryns.

They were travelling northwards again, and the players needed enough supplies to get them to Corinth.

The woman who served him was tall and fat, with huge brawny arms.

"Phew!" said Glaucus when Atticus came over with his packages. "She was large, wasn't she?"

"Yes," said Atticus. "She reminded me of the Amazon Queen, Hippolyta."

The Queen's Belt

King Eurystheus had a daughter called Admete. She was a small, scrawny, scrunched-up sort of girl with a shrill voice and a terrible temper. She was also badly spoilt, and her father gave her whatever she wanted.

One day she came to see her father, just as he was climbing out of his bronze jar.

"I want a present," she said rudely. "And I want that stupid Heracles to get it for me."

King Eurystheus smiled at her lovingly. "And what would my sweet girl like?" he asked.

"That Amazon Queen, Hippolyta. She's got a magic girdle that helps her fight. I want that so I can fight all the horrid people in this palace who laugh at me behind my back."

King Eurystheus summoned Heracles at once, and told him what his next task was to be.

Heracles couldn't help smiling behind his hand. The thought of scrawny little Admete fighting anyone was funny. But he had to do as Eurystheus wanted, so off he set for the river Thermodon, where the Amazons lived.

The Amazons were fierce women warriors who liked nothing better than a good fight. So Heracles thought he had better take all his weapons, just in case they were too strong for him.

But when he landed his boat, a huge woman came running to greet him.

"Hail, Heracles the Hero!" she said. "We have heard of your great deeds, and our queen would like to invite you to a feast in your honour."

Heracles was very surprised, but he went with the woman to the palace to meet Queen Hippolyta.

When Queen Hippolyta saw Heracles she was impressed with his size and strength. He told her all about his task, and she kindly agreed to give him her girdle as a present.

Now the goddess Hera had disguised

herself as one of the Amazons so that
she could spy on Heracles, and when she
learned of Queen Hippolyta's gift,
she was disgusted.

"So Heracles thinks this is an easy
task," she spat. "We'll just see about that!"

And off she went to spread terrible rumours that Heracles was going to kidnap Hippolyta and carry her off. This made the other Amazons very angry indeed.

As Queen Hippolyta strode down to the shore the morning after the feast to give Heracles her girdle, the Amazons mounted their horses and charged up behind her, shooting arrows as they galloped.

Heracles leapt at poor Hippolyta, seized her by the hair and tore the girdle out of her hand.

Then he fought his way through the whole army of Amazons to get back to his boat, leapt aboard and set sail at once. As soon as he got back to Tiryns, he handed the girdle over to Eurystheus, who ran to find his daughter.

"Here you are, my dearest," he said. But Admete just snatched the girdle without a word of thanks and stalked off to find someone to fight.

A terrible smell wafted from the Swamp
of Lerna. Everyone held their noses as
they hurried past.

"What was that place?" asked Glaucus
as they lit the fire that night.

"That was the swamp where the Hydra
used to live before Heracles defeated it,"
said Atticus.

"I made a brilliant Hydra mask for
one of our plays in Elis," said Georgios.

"It was really frightening. I like that
story, Atticus. Will you tell it to us tonight?"

"The minute we've eaten," said Atticus.
"I'm starving."

The Swamp Monster

For hundreds of years Hera had been protecting a dreadful monster. She thought it would be useful to have a pet monster, in case she needed it to kill someone.

So when Eurystheus was thinking up another task for Heracles, she flew down from Olympus to tell him about her Hydra, hoping that it would kill Heracles with its venomous breath.

Now the Hydra lived in a sludgy, squelchy swamp just outside the city of Lerna. It had its lair underneath a tall plane tree right in the middle, where it writhed and wriggled in and out of the filthy water, hissing and spitting horribly smelly poison from its nine snaky heads. One of its heads had a large lump of gold set into it, and it was this head which was the most dangerous, because it could never die.

When Heracles was told about this task, he was in despair.

"How ever shall I kill it?" he asked his friend Iolaus.

Iolaus didn't know, but the goddess Athene did, and as Heracles and Iolaus arrived at Lerna, she appeared beside them in their chariot.

"You'll never do this without some help," she said, "and as Hera is helping Eurystheus, I don't see why I shouldn't help you. Now, this is what you have to do."

Heracles followed Athene's advice exactly. He fired burning arrows at the monster to make it come out, and then held his breath while he tried to strangle it.

But the monster tripped him up with its scaly tail, and although he kept cutting its heads off with his sword, more and more kept growing.

Then Hera sent a huge crab to help the Hydra, and it nipped Heracles' toes till he shrieked and stamped on its shell, crushing it to death.

Iolaus saw that his friend was in trouble, so he set some branches on fire, and rushed in and burnt the stumps where Heracles had cut the Hydra's heads off. This stopped the new ones growing, and finally Heracles was able to cut the last golden head off. He carried it to the shore, and buried it, still hissing, under a great stone.

Then he dipped his arrows in the Hydra's poison, making them so dangerous that the slightest wound from

one would kill any living thing.

Because Iolaus had helped Heracles
in his task, Eurystheus said it didn't
count, and so he made Heracles do an
extra task as a punishment later on.

Hera was furious that her monstrous

pet was dead, and it made her hate Heracles more than ever. She took the crab that had helped the Hydra, and placed it among the stars, where it hangs to this very day, nipping at the heels of any who cross its path in the sky.

They had just left the town of Stymphalus when Atticus's sandal strap broke at last. He stopped to rummage for a new pair in Melissa's pack.

"It seems ages since I sat down and made these back in Crete," he said. "I wonder how they're all getting on. Just think of all the places we've seen already, and how far we've still got to go." He gave a big sigh and Melissa blew through her whiskers.

Just then Glaucus gave a shout and pointed ahead. A flock of white ibises had flown up from the marsh to their right.

As they flew towards the sunset,
their wings turned pink and gold.

"Perhaps those are the famous
Stymphalian Birds," said Atticus as he
caught up with the others. "But I do
hope not." And he began to tell them
all the tale as they walked.

Bronze Feathers

After Heracles had caught the Hind
of Ceryneia, King Eurystheus
couldn't think of anything dangerous
enough for him to do.

Then a messenger came from the
people of a village called Stymphalus, to
say that they had been invaded by a flock
of dreadful birds, which had flown down
from the north, and had settled in the
nearby marsh. They had sharp feathers of
bronze which they plucked out and
threw at people, wounding them terribly.

"Go and get me some of those bronze
feathers immediately. They'll make a nice
crown for me to wear at the next feast,"

ordered Eurystheus, who was vain as well as cowardly. "You can drive the birds away for the villagers as well."

Heracles arrived in Stymphalus at dawn. The villagers took him to the marsh, where the birds were all roosting in a huge flock in the very middle. As the sun rose, it flashed off their bright feathers, and all the villagers ran away in terror.

 48

Heracles started to shoot his arrows at the birds, but they were too far away, and the arrows fell uselessly on the boggy ground.

"Looks like you need some help again, my friend," said a voice beside him.

When Heracles turned round, there was Athene, standing laughing at him and holding a great big rattle which Hephaestus the blacksmith god had made for her.

"This will make enough noise to scare those birds away for ever, and you can pick up some feathers for that stupid Eurystheus when they've gone. If you tread carefully you won't sink much in the marsh, and you can collect your precious arrows at the same time."

Heracles thanked Athene, and blocked up his ears with wax to shut out the noise.

Then he started
to swing the rattle.

Whirr-a-
whirrrr-a-
whirrrr-
a-wheeee

it went,
and the birds
rose straight
into the air,
screeching with terror, and flew off.

As they flew, their feathers cascaded
down in showers, and the ground
glittered as if it was covered with bronze-
coloured snow.

Heracles picked the feathers up one
by one, careful not to cut his fingers on
the sharp edges, and put them into a
stout sack.

When he got back to Tiryns, he tipped the sack out at Eurystheus's feet.

"Ooh! Lovely!" squealed Eurystheus, grabbing at the feathers as they fell.

But he was soon sorry for his greed as he dabbed at his cut and bleeding fingers.

As for the Stymphalian Birds, they never stopped flying till they reached the Isle of Ares in the Black Sea. And there they lived in peace until a ship full of heroes landed there and chased them away, and they were never heard of again.

At last the players reached Corinth. They had soon found work, and now Glaucus was dancing round Melissa.

"They liked us, Atticus! The Council of Corinth has offered us a permanent post at the amphitheatre!" he shouted. "I can send for my wife and children, and we can get a little house."

"This calls for a celebration story!" Atticus exclaimed, clapping his hands. "What would you like tonight? I'm off to find a boat to Calydon early in the morning, so this will be our last night together."

Glaucus didn't even need to think about it. "It has to be Heracles' last task," he said, beaming. And off he went to arrange a magnificent feast.

The Guardian
of the Underworld

Heracles' last task was his most difficult yet.

"Go and fetch me the fearsome dog Cerberus, who guards the gates of Tartarus," squeaked Eurystheus from the safety of his bronze jar. He knew Heracles wouldn't be very pleased.

"Very well, you wretched little man," growled Heracles. "But don't blame me if you're so scared when you see him that you don't come out from that jar for a whole year!"

The entrance to the Underworld was very hard to find, and Heracles spent a long time looking for it. He found it at last, but he was in a terrible temper as he climbed down the dark, dark passages to Hades' kingdom.

When he reached the river Styx, he aimed an arrow at the old boatman, Charon.

"Take me across, or else," he shouted, and as he stepped into the wobbly boat, Charon started rowing as fast as he could.

The ghosts on the far side twittered and rustled as he brushed through them, and although he stopped to talk to one or two old friends, Heracles was still in a bad mood.

Hades himself trembled at the look on Heracles' face when he marched up to the outer gates of the palace.

"Give me that dog," Heracles demanded, pointing at the horrid three-headed dog growling by the gate.

The dog's heads and back were covered with a mane of writhing snakes, its teeth were as long as spears and it had a lashing serpent's tail. Its great round eyes were as big as cartwheels, and redder than rubies.

Hades bowed and rubbed his hands together. "Take him with pleasure," he said.

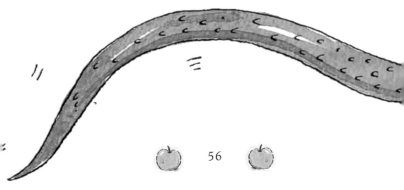

"But you mustn't use your arrows or club."

"Fine!" said Heracles grimly, and he put on the armour he had made from the skin of the Nemean lion.

Then he started to wrestle with Cerberus. What a great fight it was. Cerberus bit with all three mouths, and his snake mane hissed and spat, but Heracles hung on and on and on until Cerberus gave up and lay down, all four paws pointing to the dark sky above.

Heracles dragged him up to earth, and threw him out of the door of the Underworld into the light of day.

Cerberus whimpered as the bright sunshine hit his eyes, and then he started

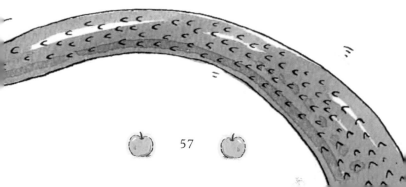

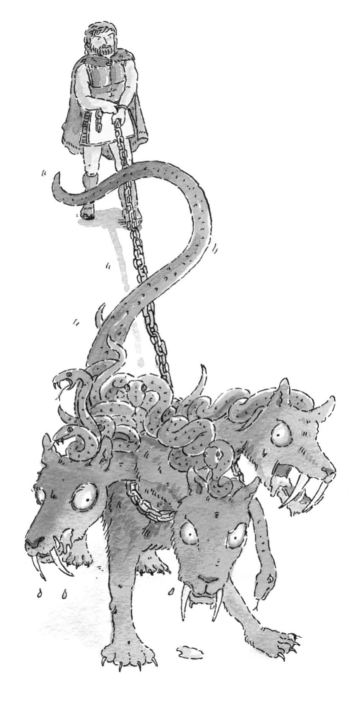

to bark. Great drops of slobber flew from his jaws, and as they landed on the fields, they turned into the poisonous yellow flowers we call aconites.

Heracles took a huge chain made of the hardest diamonds from his pocket, and tied it round Cerberus's neck. Then he pulled him all the way to the palace at Tiryns.

Eurystheus took one look at the terrifying beast, and fainted back into his jar.

As Heracles had prophesied, he didn't come out for a whole year, and even then he trembled so much that he couldn't eat more than a mouthful at a time.

Heracles didn't know what to do with Cerberus, so he took him back to Tartarus and gave him back to Hades. His twelve tasks were finished and he was a free man at last.

Zeus was proud of his fine son, and vowed that one day he should come and live on Olympus.

But Heracles travelled round Greece for many more years before that happened, performing greater and greater deeds until there was no one in the whole world who had not heard of Heracles the Hero.

The next morning Atticus and Melissa said goodbye to the players and went down to the harbour. They had to find a ship to take them across the bay to Calydon.

As they walked into the busy port, there seemed to be hundreds to choose from.

"If only you had wings like Pegasus, Melissa, then we could fly," sighed Atticus. "But I suppose we'll have to go and bargain for our passage."

As they waited in line to speak to the captain of a likely looking ship, Atticus sat down on the quay, his legs dangling. To pass the time, he decided to tell Melissa a story.

The Flying Horse

Bellerophon was the grandson of King Sisyphus Sharp-Eyes, and he had only one dream in his life – to ride on the back of the great winged horse, Pegasus. When the hero Perseus had cut off the Gorgon Medusa's head, the blood from her body had run into the sand.

Later that night a beautiful winged horse had been born, and the gods had named him Pegasus, and decreed that he could only be ridden by a great hero. Bellerophon was determined that that hero was going to be him.

When Bellerophon was staying with King Iobates of Lycia, the king asked him a great favour. Iobates had a terrible enemy, the king of Caria, who had a pet monster, the Chimaera. This monster had a lion's body, a goat's head and a snake's tail, and the king of Caria had sent it into Lycia to destroy his enemy's army with its fiery breath.

"If you could only kill the monster," begged King Iobates. "Then my poor soldiers would be saved, and you would be a great hero."

Now Bellerophon wanted to be a hero very much, but he had no idea how to kill a Chimaera. So he went to consult an oracle.

"First you must catch the winged horse, Pegasus, as he drinks at the Spring of Peirene in Corinth. Then you must tame him with Athene's golden bridle before you can ride him to destroy the monster," said the oracle.

Bellerophon was delighted, but how was he to get a golden bridle from Athene?

He travelled to Corinth, and lay down by the spring to sleep. But before he closed his eyes, he prayed for Athene's help.

That night he had a strange dream. A tall woman with a winged helmet and wise grey eyes took him by the hand and pointed to a bush with spiky green leaves. It was Athene, and underneath the bush was a beautiful golden bridle.

Early the next morning Bellerophon was woken by the hooting of an owl.

He sat bolt upright, and there, right in front of him, was the spiky green bush he had seen in his dream! He ran over to it and pulled out the golden bridle just as Pegasus flew down to drink. As the soaring white wings folded, Bellerophon threw the bridle over Pegasus's head and leaped onto his back.

"To Caria," he cried, and Pegasus sprang into the air and started to fly eastwards.

Soon they saw a haze of sooty smoke beneath them, and heard the sounds of fighting.

Bellerophon fired arrow after arrow at the monstrous Chimaera until it roared and danced with pain. Then Pegasus swooped low enough for him to thrust a spear with a lump of lead on the end into its mouth.

The Chimaera bit the spear in its rage, and swallowed it, and the lead melted in the heat of its fiery throat and trickled down inside its stomach, killing it instantly.

King Iobates was delighted and insisted that Bellerophon should marry his daughter and be king after him. But soon Bellerophon longed to ride Pegasus again. One summer's morning he bridled him, and climbed onto his back.

"Fly, Pegasus, fly! Fly to Olympus so that I may see the gods in their palaces!" he cried proudly.

Zeus heard him and was angry. He sent a gadfly to sting Pegasus under the tail so that he reared and threw Bellerophon down to earth. Pegasus himself flew on to Olympus, where Zeus now uses him to carry his thunderbolts around the heavens.

But proud Bellerophon landed in a prickly thornbush, and Zeus made him wander the world, lame and blind, for the rest of his wretched life.

The sea was calm, and Atticus and Melissa
sniffed the salty breeze as they sailed away
from Corinth. Just then Atticus felt a tug
on his purse. A small boy was trying to
loosen it.

"Oi," said Atticus. "Are you trying to
rob me?"

The boy looked up with scared eyes.

"I expect you're hungry, is that it?"

The boy nodded.

"If you promise not to steal again, I'll
tell you a story and give you something to
eat," said Atticus.

The boy promised, and they settled
down together on deck with some bread
and olives while Atticus told a story.

The Cunning Thief

Autolycus, son of the messenger god Hermes, lived on the Isthmus of Corinth, and he was a cattle thief. But he wasn't just an ordinary cattle thief – no, he was the best and most cunning cattle thief ever born.

His father Hermes had given him the gift of transforming whatever beasts he stole, from black to white, or from white to black; from red to yellow or from yellow to red; from horned to unhorned and from unhorned to horned. Whatever beast he stole, he could always disguise it so that not even its mother would have known which it was.

Now Autolycus lived right next door to King Sisyphus Sharp-Eyes, who had a fine fat herd of cattle which he was very proud of.

Every night and every day, a cow or two or a prize bull would disappear from Sisyphus's herd, and although he knew it must be Autolycus who was stealing them because his herds were growing bigger every week, even Sisyphus's sharp eyes couldn't spot how he was doing it.

One hot dusty day, King Sisyphus counted up his cattle and found he had just six fine red bulls and twenty fine white cows left.

"I shall lay a trap for Autolycus," he said to his cowherds, "which will catch him once and for all."

And he did. He took each cow and each bull's left hoof and carved the words "Stolen by Autolycus" in very small letters inside each one. Then he sat and waited.

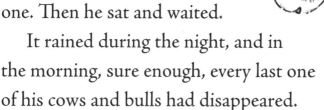

It rained during the night, and in the morning, sure enough, every last one of his cows and bulls had disappeared.

Calling on his friends as witnesses, he followed the trail of marked footprints through the mud and right to the door of Autolycus's house.

"Caught you at last, thief!" he cried.

And Autolycus had to give all Sisyphus's cattle back to him.

As Autolycus was turning Sisyphus's cattle back to their right colours, Sisyphus caught sight of Autolycus's daughter. He fell in love with her, and later she bore him a son called Odysseus, who went on to become a great hero – and even more cunning than his father and grandfather put together!

Greek Beasts and Heroes and where to find them...

The stories of all Heracles' other exciting adventures can be found in *The Fire Breather* and *The Harp of Death* in this series.

"The Girl Who Ran Fastest" was tricked by some more of those dangerous golden apples! Atalanta's story is in *The Harp of Death*.

Do you think the Stymphalian birds would be just too frightening to meet? For a happier story of soft white swan feathers – and love – look for *The Silver Chariot* and turn to the story called "Rainbow Eggs".

Having read about Bellerophon, you'll definitely want to read about his cunning grandfather Sisyphus. "The Sharp-Eyed King" will tell you all you want to know, and it's in *The Dolphin's Message*.

Autolycus was a cunning thief, no doubt
about it. But perhaps the youngest thief in
the **Greek Beasts and Heroes** books is
Hermes. Find out what he stole in "The
Baby and the Cows" in *The Silver Chariot*.

Greek Beasts and Heroes
have you read them all?